Helping Mom

Also by Jane M. Mayer

Self-Care from Body to Bliss
The Accidental Caregiver Series
Helping Others Without Losing Yourself

Helping Mom

The Accidental Caregiver Series

Helping Others Without Losing Yourself

Jane M. Mayer

SWEET JANE LLC

2024

Helping Mom
The Accidental Caregiver Series
Helping Others Without Losing Yourself
Jane M. Mayer

This book provides general information and discussions
about health and related subjects. The information and other
content provided in this book, or in any linked materials, are
not intended and should not be construed as medical or legal
advice, nor is the information a substitute for professional
medical expertise or treatment.

Editor: Stacey Dyck
Cover/Book Design: Margi Levitt

Published by Sweet Jane LLC • www.sweetjaneslife.com
ISBN: 979-8-9900080-0-7 (ebook)
ISBN: 979-8-9900080-1-4 (paperback)

To all the selfless souls of the world,
thank you for your kindness and for showing up
when it matters most.

Contents

Introduction

THIS GUIDE WAS INSPIRED BY my experience caregiving for my aging mother, in our family home, for six years. It draws on the practical and personal insights I gained during this time, not to mention the many lessons learned. It's also meant to inspire some hope, as these years with my mom enriched my life in many unexpected but wonderful ways.

Are you considering looking after an aging loved one and searching for ways to manage this new stage of life? I see you and I've got you.

This life choice takes an inordinate amount of time and energy, both physically and emotionally. What often happens is that the routine unfolds, your own individual and personal needs start to be neglected, and you soon find yourself depleted and resentful.

It is possible, however, to step up in this important way while preserving your own physical, mental, emotional, and spiritual well-being. I know because I've lived it and I managed to weather these years well enough that others who witnessed my experience started to contemplate caring for their own family members and seeking out my advice.

Every situation is different, but I hope that in reading this guide, you feel gently supported and understood by someone who knows what you're going through and has some tips and tricks on how to make it through.

"When we feel love and
kindness toward others,
it not only makes others feel
loved and cared for,
but it helps us also to
develop inner happiness
and peace."

– DALAI LAMA

1

Explore All Options

TO ANYONE WHO SEEKS my counsel and tells me that they plan to take on the responsibility of caring for one of their parents at home, I respond with an emphatic, "Explore all other options before you engage!!".

This might seem like strange advice in a caregiving how-to, but if there is any another choice, do that instead. Whether it is a small group home or hiring a professional in-home caregiver, give it every consideration.

I know that these options, including assisted living centers, can be prohibitively expensive. I also know that you probably feel like no one will love and care for your person as well as you can. But my sweet friend, a caregiving relationship is not for the faint of heart and can require superhuman levels of patience. If there is any professional avenue to take on the "heavy lifting" (which, in this case, is not just a metaphor), I suggest you go that way and then you can use your time and energy to be your person's constant and supportive beacon of love and light.

That said, if you are reading this, it is very likely that you've already made the choice to take on the herculean task of being an Accidental Caregiver. And like I said before, I'm here for you.

Let's get started...

"There are only four kinds
of people in the world:
those who have been caregivers,
those who are currently caregivers,
those who will be caregivers, and
those who will need a caregiver."

– ROSALYN CARTER

Set Your Intentions

ONCE I MADE THE DECISION to take my mom into our home and become her permanent caregiver, the first thing I did was set my intentions. This may sound unnecessary as my intention seems pretty clear – to take care of Mom to the best of my ability.

Intentions are key to achieving goals as they can provide a road map for what is to come and can inform future choices and timelines. Being upfront and honest with one another about our intentions allowed me to be clear about where I believed my 'edge' to be.

Let me explain…

I told Mom when she moved in that I was up to the task of taking care of her at home as long as she could manage her own toileting. "When that changes," I said, "I will need to call in reinforcements or we will have to make other arrangements."

Stating my intention helped Mom:

Understand what was expected of her and it gave her a 'heads up' as to how things might progress in the future. It was also motivating for her to continue trying in this regard because she wanted to stay with us for as long as possible.

Stating my intention helped me:

Acknowledge my abilities, and perceived inabilities, with having to help her use the bathroom. It was important to give myself permission to operate within that boundary or edge.

In my case, these bathroom boundaries were eventually challenged, and wouldn't you know it, I rose to the occasion. I've come to understand that this Accidental Caregiver lifestyle, and all associated intentions and best laid plans, will start one way and inevitably evolve (or, unfortunately, devolve) into something quite different. It became increasingly important to be flexible and understanding – both with myself and Mom – and willing to make lots of adjustments along the way.

Strategy #1 – Set Intentions

- *Think through your personal intentions for being an Accidental Caregiver for your person.*

- *Communicate them clearly to your person. You may want to write them down together in a way that captures agreement.*

- *Ask them to think through and share their intentions.*

- *Listen carefully and accept their intentions wholeheartedly, even if it doesn't match what you want for them.*

- *Establish clearly what you need from each other to uphold and honor each other's edge.*

"Caring is the bridge
that connects us to one another."

– THICH NHAT HANH

3

Acknowledge Your Skills

HAVING ALREADY LEARNED through other life experiences what it takes to be an Accidental Caregiver, I assumed that my love for my mom and my nurturing personality would be enough to carry me through. As it turns out, those are the barest of baselines to achieve success in this role. Taking responsibility for nearly every aspect of another adult's well-being requires an entire catalog of skills – some I had, some that I needed to learn and some that felt completely beyond me.

Personal Skills Assessment: Part 1

In planning for Mom to join us, I realized that I had better do an inventory of how my personal skills stacked up against the responsibilities I was taking on. In doing this, I was quickly reminded that I am, in fact, NOT a: *nurse, gastroenterologist, nutritionist, natural pathologist, dermatologist, podiatrist, pedicure/manicure technician, professional shopper, banker, lawyer, hair stylist, massage therapist or AV support technician.*

And yet, here I was assuming each of these roles to one degree or another, with the job descriptions expanding exponentially as time passed, especially once Mom became housebound.

If your person is mobile, willing, and there is the financial ability to do so, much of this can be handled by professionals. We were able to rely on these professionals for a while, but as Mom became more and more immobile, it came down to me. Who knew I could give such a great haircut? What a discovery to learn I can treat dermatitis! Internet research, phone calls to the experts, and a whole lot of trial and error, were all just part of the process of my becoming a Jane-of-all-trades for Mom's every need.

Personal Skills Assessment: Part 2

The second part of my personal skills inventory involved me reminding myself of all the strengths and skills I do bring to the table. I may not be a gastroenterologist, but I AM or have been, at one time or another, a:

mother, daughter, sister, wife, good friend, teacher, yoga instructor, writer, advertising TV producer, server, cook, baker, life coach, event planner and business owner.

Throughout my life, I have also been recognized for my ability to care and nurture, and while that's not enough on its own, it was still an important part of the equation. It was also important and validating for me to recognize the value of my strengths and remind myself that I had spent my life building a pretty stellar 'toolbox' of skills for me to draw on.

There are two people in a caregiving relationship, however, and sometimes what one person considers an asset, the other sees as an annoyance. An example of this is how my believing the glass is always half full and every cloud has a silver lining, became a source of friction for me and my mom.

I pride myself on not allowing negativity to creep into my life, and I actively avoid falling prey to the 'victim mentality'. Mom was not of the same mind. It was far more comfortable and familiar for her to provide a running report on all that was wrong in her world, and to complain and lay blame at regular intervals. I would listen as best I could, silently wishing she could just acknowledge all that was in her favor. This was a consistent source of pain in our relationship until I decided to try and see things from her point of view. It was with this in mind that one day, I responded to her complaints with, "It must feel awful to be trapped in your own body". Her face lit up a little and she agreed, "Yes, yes, it does." I think in that moment she felt seen and understood, and consequently was able to see me as an ally, as well as an aide.

How could I know what it felt like to be aged and marginalized, made smaller by the world around you, and outliving your spouse and all your friends? I hadn't experienced what it is to lose your independence and freedom, along with the knowledge that the future only holds a narrowing and uncertain path. I couldn't draw on my own experiences, so I knew that I had to try and see things from her perspective more often. This meant that my job entailed more than making meals and getting her medications, it required accessing a deep well of compassion for what she was going through. I'll admit that my brand of sympathy was still likely less coddling and cooing,

"You poor thing…" as she might have liked, but I did my best in my own way.

Although I worked to tailor my approach to better suit her needs, I knew that I had to still be authentic and aligned with both my natural tendencies and unique skill set. The relationship between a mother and daughter is a richly complex one and so sometimes what I had to offer was enough, and sometimes it wasn't. We both learned to live with that. Thankfully there were other people in our lives who were able to provide her with the attention and deference that she needed.

It is important for us Accidental Caregivers to remember that even though we may not have the training or professional credentials to be doing the jobs we take on, we do have a lifetime of experience and learned skills in our toolboxes. It serves us well to consider how we can translate those unique strengths into helping us navigate this challenging adventure.

❧

Strategy #1 – Set Intentions

- *Think about and list all the skills and abilities that you bring to the table. Be as thorough as possible and remember that there is value in every experience and life lesson learned.*

- *Consider how those skills align with the typical tasks required of caregivers and identify any gaps.*

- *Make a plan for how you can access professionals, resources, friends and family, to share the load and take on the jobs that suit their strengths and abilities*

- *Have fun with this! It's affirming to write down all your accomplishments and spend a minute celebrating all you've done. Seeing the success you've achieved in other areas of your life may also bolster your confidence that you can do this too.*

"The most painful thing
is losing yourself in the
process of loving someone
too much, and forgetting
that you are special too."

– ERNEST HEMINGWAY

4

Create a Schedule

I'm A PLANNER. My career has included many jobs that require extensive prepping and a high degree of organization, and it's just in my nature to get things done. Given this, you may be surprised to hear that I did not create a detailed schedule when I first started caregiving for my mom, but I sure wish I had.

If you are a parent, you likely already understand the value of a schedule. A baby without a consistent routine is like a human game of Perfection. You run around trying to fit everything into irregular shaped spaces, while often having the entire thing blow up in your face. Good times.

A set schedule and predictable routine creates a sense of safety and security for people of any age. It's especially important for those who are aging or failing, as it helps them know what is expected of them, gives them a sense of control as they know what happens next, and can help to break up the very long days and weeks.

For the caregiver, it allows you to maintain some semblance of a life outside of your caregiving duties. By having a consistent time set aside when you know that you will unplug from your responsibilities and get away (or even just get to be alone), you give yourself something to look forward to and a way to combat the feelings of overwhelm and endlessness. Scheduling time for yourself is so important but it's not easy. Even knowing all of this, I could have done a much better job prioritizing my needs at times along the way.

People treat you the way you allow them to, so if you are constantly at someone's beck and call, they will come to assume and expect this. Without a schedule, Mom got used to me catering to her every whim and demand. So much so, that if I chose to go away for the weekend, she became fearful and completely thrown by not having 24/7 access to me. This wasn't good for either of us. It was up to me to set some boundaries and communicate them clearly – boundaries that would have been easier to set, and likely been better received, if I had established them from the start.

Eventually, we did get onto a more regular schedule, although admittedly it was one that developed somewhat organically over the natural course of time. It was dictated primarily by Mom's sleep patterns and scheduled visits by friends, support staff and eventually the hospice nurses. Creating a routine and rhythm that allowed for Mom's changing needs made for a much smoother operation.

Strategy #3 – Set Your Schedule

- *Set aside certain days for even the most basic events, like "shower day," "getting fresh air day," "shopping day", etc.*

- *Have the calendar in a shared area that is highly visible to your person.*

- *Be clear and committed about your personal time and "days off". You don't just deserve it, you need it.*

- *Using the schedule to dictate events or activities makes it less about you telling them that something has to happen (which can create resistance) and more because the schedule 'says so'.*

"Caring for others
is the highest expression
of humanity."

– HARRIET BEECHER STOWE

5

Engage Resources

JUST BECAUSE YOU CAN DO SOMETHING on your own, doesn't mean you should. Accidental caregiving is a challenging, exhausting and often thankless job, but there are people and services to help. You will serve both yourself and your person much better if you reach out to the many available resources.

Professional Caregiving Services

Depending on where you live, there is a good chance that there are reputable caregiving companies in your area. These organizations, like A Place for Mom, provide free personalized guidance and will answer any questions you have. Whether you need help connecting with an occasional sitter to come and give you a break or are looking to learn where you can purchase in-home medical equipment, they're there to help.

Social Workers and Volunteers

There are community organizations and social services, as well as church and synagogue groups, that focus specifically on supporting caregivers. There are teams of volunteers willing to help your person get to appointments, do their shopping, and stay engaged in the world around them. It's so great to see a young volunteer connect with a senior, whether it's reading to them, playing cards or just visiting and exchanging ideas, while their caregiver takes a much-needed break. A win-win-win.

Mental Health Professionals

These professionals are essential resources for both people in a caregiving relationship. Your person has many thoughts and feelings around their situation, likely including (but certainly not limited to) grief over the loss of their abilities, loneliness after possibly outliving their spouse and friends, and a growing fear of death. You, as Accidental Caregiver, often become the repository for all those feelings – which simply pile on top of all the emotions and thoughts you yourself are experiencing. Attending talk therapy – either in-person or virtually – can help to ease suffering and provide a much-needed pressure release. Alternatively, faith-based representatives, like a minister or rabbi, are often willing to make home visits. No matter which avenue you choose, be sure to maintain a regular schedule of appointments for both you and your person.

Friends and Family

This is a tricky one. Even though there are likely people in your life that love you and love your person, they have not signed up to be Accidental Caregivers and may have a hard time getting involved. In all honesty, they may not even want to hear about it. Talking about how to find the right size of adult diapers is not a sexy conversation. This job can be a very lonely operation. That said, it will serve you well to identify your most likely allies and to be brave enough to confide in them and ask if they would be willing to help. The best approach to this is to give them a specific job that needs to be done on a regular basis. Then, as hard as it may be, hold them accountable from the start so that it becomes an ingrained part of everyone's routine.

You will likely be inundated with offers from well-intentioned friends and family asking you to "let me know if I can do anything." Granted this is sometimes lip service, but there will be people who genuinely want to help but don't know how. Take these people up on their offers and ask for what you need.

Strategy #4 – Accept Help

Specific ways that friends and family can help your person:

- *Text, email and call. Loneliness is real.*

- *Send cards or letters in the mail.*

- *Share photographs of life activities.*

- *Schedule short visits.*

- *Drop off little treats or small gifts. Older people often think they are not worthy of presents anymore because they may not be around long enough to enjoy them.*

Specific ways that friends and family can help you:

- *Text, email and call. The feeling of isolation that caregiving brings is as real as the loneliness.*

- *Create a non-judgmental space to listen.*

- *Visit and do something joyful, like watching fun TV or even just chatting over snacks and drinks. There can be a lot of heaviness involved in caregiving and intentionally injecting some lightness can go a long way.*

Entertainment

If your person is home-bound for a long period like my mom was, they likely spend most of their time in bed or in a recliner. Mom once spent hours reading and knitting but eventually her eyes made these pastimes impossible. Instead, she ended up watching a lot of TV. I was able to subscribe to a few extra streaming channels that interested her, which helped to keep her entertained and occupied. As her hearing declined, we set her up with headphones which helped for quite a while.

Luckily for both of us, my mom was very adept at using her iPhone. We added apps and paid the nominal fees so that she could play endless hours of games, like Solitaire, without being bothered by ads. These simple little additions added up to big distractions and gave us both much needed reprieves.

She was also able to plug in her headphones and enjoy her favorite music. Music is medicine for the soul at any age, but for the elderly, it can help keep the brain engaged and be a soothing remedy to boredom and despair. Mom and I created a robust playlist of the classics and her favorites from years gone by. Audio books can also be a nice alternative to TV. There are many apps that provide access to these, and your local library likely has thousands of free audio books available for download.

"Remember always that
you not only have the
right to be an individual,
you have an obligation
to be one."

– ELEANOR ROOSEVELT

6

Things to Consider

THE LEARNING CURVE OF BECOMING an Accidental Caregiver is steep and my first few months with Mom felt like an endless discovery of things I hadn't considered or challenges I hadn't anticipated. Below are just some aspects of caregiving that you may want to prepare yourself and your person for.

BATHROOM

This aspect of caregiving is often one that carries a significant amount of trepidation, on both people's part. The bathroom also represents physical safety challenges that need to be managed.

We adapted Mom's bathroom to accommodate her aging needs with:

Roll-in shower with a curtain

Handrail in the shower

Shower chair

Handrail adjacent to the toilet

High-sitting toilet

Wide enough space to fit a walker

As previously mentioned, the bathroom was one area that I had to set an intention around. Having tended to my dad in his last days of pancreatic cancer, I knew that toileting could become both a physically and emotionally fraught experience for us both. From the beginning, I was clear with Mom that as long as she could get herself to and from the bathroom on her own, I could manage our situation.

Ah, best laid plans. Even though we were committed to a self-reliant bathroom experience, accidents and emergencies happen and adult diapers became a necessity. Humility comes in large doses when you take on the role of caregiver, but I admit that I still felt the need to let the checkout person know that the packs of diapers weren't for me! Eventually I learned that purchasing them in bulk from an online provider was both cost-effective and less embarrassing. Mom ended up wearing them daily as underpants, which was expensive but seemed like a small price to pay for the emotional and physical sense of security they provide.

BEDROOM

Your person's bedroom is an important space as it is likely where they will spend a good portion of their time.

1. If it's feasible to invest in an adjustable bed, do so. We didn't have one, but I know that pressing a button to help Mom sit up, or to lift her legs to help with circulation, would have been far easier than our searching for the right combination of pillows, backrests and bolsters. As you can raise and lower the mattress on these beds, they make it

easier for your person to get in and out of bed, which increases their independence.

2. A good quality mattress, mattress topper, and a waterproof mattress liner are all essential for comfort and easy clean-up. Soft sheets will also promote comfort – just be sure to wash new sets multiple times before using and always wash bedding in detergent that is safe for sensitive skin.

3. A lamp on the nightstand with a 3-way bulb is a nice addition, as it provides three different levels of light to best suit what's happening in the room. Mom's room also had battery operated candles that she loved being able to turn on and off with the little remote control.

4. A window with a screen allows much-needed fresh air into the room and brings a bit of the outside in. I put a hummingbird feeder outside Mom's window, atop a shrub with bright orange flowers, to add some cheer and the possibility of some nature sightings. Fresh flowers and living plants in the room add oxygen and color, and can help to lift spirits and make the environment more pleasing to be in.

5. At Mom's insistence, we kept a flashlight in her nightstand. She said she wanted one in case she dropped something at night, and it was an easy way to enhance her sense of security.

6. Seating in the room is important as you will also spend lots of time in there, as will any visitors and additional aides.

7. We had lots of pictures, mementos and art decorating the walls of Mom's room. These can remind your person of happy times and memories, and help them feel more tethered

to the world. You may want to swap new ones in on a regular basis, as they will likely prompt the same stories to be told again and again. Patience is a virtue for the Accidental Caregiver, but there are things we can do to help ourselves.

EMOTIONAL SUPPORT

As your person's primary caregiver, you will also be their most significant source of emotional support. Everyone is different in terms of the type of emotional support they want and need but for us, it involved:

- Listening. Lots and lots of listening. Like many older people, Mom tended to loop back to the same stories again and again. It seemed to help reinforce a sense of relevance and may have reflected the very human need to make sense of what happened in one's past. I tried to validate her feelings as much as possible, and sometimes tried to gently re-direct or re-frame her thinking to consider to an alternative perspective that might open new possibilities of acceptance for the situation at hand.

- Seniors receive the least amount of physical contact, at a time when it is increasingly important for their sense of well-being. Holding my mom's hand and making sure to give her lots of hugs and loving touches, became a way for me to express warmth, concern, security, encouragement, and comfort.

- As someone's world becomes smaller and smaller, the events of the day start to take on (what can seem to us) disproportionate significance. This could include obsessing over something as small as a hangnail or perseverating about an incident that occurred months before. I tried to remember that with so few novel experiences in her life, what seemed inconsequential to me were actually very big for Mom.

LEGAL ISSUES

This is a highly complex topic, and I am far from an expert. I will share our experience dealing with matters of guardianship, finances and power of attorney, but be sure to reach out to legal counsel early and often.

If possible, it is very important to get your person's 'affairs in order' while they are still of sound mind and body. These conversations are never easy to initiate or wade through, but gather your courage and dive in. I guarantee that you will be happy in the long run that you did.

There are good reasons to make estate-related decisions sooner than later. Life can turn on a dime, and you never know what tomorrow will bring. Being prepared helps everyone sleep a little better knowing that there is a clear path forward no matter what scenario presents itself.

Another reason to be proactive about this is that grief-stricken family and friends are not exactly the best decision-makers. When my dad was in his final days, I took time off and flew home to be with him and my mom. Immediately after he passed, we were confronted with so many decisions and logistical hurdles. We were having to discuss caskets and cremains while our heads were spinning with sadness, not to mention hunting through file boxes for insurance plans, paying bills, closing accounts, and trying to think about all the people we needed to contact. It would have been really helpful if we had been better prepared and able to complete the needed tasks without the stress and scrambling.

Having these end-of-life conversations beforehand also means that everyone is clear about 'who is getting the fine china' or whatever that might be for your family. Clarifying and codifying your person's wishes in advance will take the onus off you, as Accidental Caregiver, when it comes time to divvy up the estate.

Mom used to randomly declare what she wanted to have happen with her things. "I want Rose to get my opal jewelry!" she'd say somewhat out of the blue. I'd encourage her to write it down and reassured her that I would make sure that things happened just as she wanted. In my mom's case, her assets were very small and didn't warrant getting an estate lawyer involved. She would just write it down, date and sign it, I'd witness it and we would file it away. If your person has significant assets or bequests, it's a good idea to have their wishes legally documented and notarized.

There are three legal areas that, even if you do nothing else to prepare, you should have in place as soon as possible after assuming caregiving responsibilities. There are estate planners and lawyers who specialize in elder care who can walk you through each of these. There is, of course, a cost to this but take it from me, running around trying to piece-meal different documents and plans together is not the way to go. Ah well, live and learn.

Medical Directive

Also known as a Living Will, this is a formal declaration of what medical measures your person wants to be taken should a life-threatening event occur. My mom wanted a Do Not Resuscitate order in place. This directive, often referred to as a DNR, indicates to doctors and other healthcare providers that CPR is not to be attempted if the person's heart stops beating. There are many versions and variations of this directive, so it is best to seek professional advice from your primary doctor or attorney. It is important that this document be kept in a safe place, where it is easily accessible. A copy of the DNR should be posted on the wall in your person's room so everyone is informed and aware.

Power of Attorney and Medical Power of Attorney

Even before Mom came to live with us, I assumed both power of attorney, and medical power of attorney, for her. We made this decision together, filled out the forms and had them notarized.

A power of attorney is a legal document that gives someone else the right, while you are still alive, to act on your behalf with respect to your financial affairs, including debts. Medical power of attorney is a legal document that gives someone legal authority to make important decisions about your medical care. These decisions could be about treatment options, medication, surgery, end-of-life care, and more.

Both 'powers' came in very handy as Mom became less able to manage her affairs and relied on me to make appointments, stay on top of her medications, etc. Having these in place meant that when I was asked by doctors and bankers if I was authorized to make decisions, the answer was an easy "yes".

The mental and emotional aspect of your person willingly relinquishing power over their decision-making can be a challenge. Ideally any power of attorney is backed by a relationship of trust and a stated commitment to remain collaborative and transparent for as long as possible. Having these conversations while life is in a stable place, and not in the throes of panic and crisis, will serve you both well. With any luck, your person will understand the value of the arrangement and come to see it as less of a 'takeover' and more of a proactive 'fall back'.

One thing that helped me and Mom immensely is that early on, we established a joint bank account. She maintained her personal checking account, but the joint account meant that I had access to funds to cover the items and services I managed on her behalf. Again, this arrangement requires a good deal of trust and a shared belief that you are always acting with their best interest in mind.

Some families, especially if there are multiple siblings or close family members involved, decide to assign the medical power of attorney to more than one person. This can get tricky. Unless everyone is on exactly the same page (which is rare), it's likely better to make the tough decision upfront and have just one person in the position of final say.

I've witnessed more than once what can happen when the power of attorney isn't clearly defined. Emotions run high, the fear of death creeps in, agreement can't be reached, and medical decisions are agonized over and prolonged. The division this causes can be detrimental to a family, sometimes permanently.

Holding tough conversations and making hard decisions is an act of deep compassion that will go a long way in helping your family properly honor and come together in your person's last days.

Material Possessions

When Mom moved in with us, she went from her apartment into our detached casita. This meant that we were fortunately able to bring her most prized possessions, including some of her furniture and art. Keepsakes were sorted and stored in bins in our garage, and the photo albums were kept in the living area.

While it all sounds positive on paper, this move was surprisingly stressful. Even though Mom was happy to be living with us, this transition drove home the fact that her independence was waning and the fear of being marginalized and discounted really took over. I was not ready for this reaction. At all. I went into it expecting her to be light and relaxed, not to mention maybe grateful (!) for all the work we had done selling her old place and making her new home safe and comfortable. Instead, I quickly realized that she was still reeling from the downsizing process that we'd gone through to get to this stage.

As we were packing her up, I remember standing at her closet while she sat on the bed, and we reviewed each article of clothing in her closet. It was excruciating. Each article of clothing had a story and the decision to keep, donate, or toss a given item, did not come easily. This was hard, and harder still because as she struggled to decide, I could easily see what could and should be purged. My mom is not someone who loves change. We repeated this process again and again, whether it was with old VHS tapes, kitchenware she didn't need, and a million other possessions gathered over her lifetime.

For as much as I worked with her and tried to keep her involved in the process, I also did a lot of sorting, tossing, donating, storing, cleaning, and organizing her things on my own. I thought this would be seen as doing her a favor, but she had experienced it as being disrespected or left out of the process. Whoops – another lesson learned. It took me a minute to fully understand this reaction and get over my expectation for unbridled appreciation, but eventually I did come to see that this move, while positive and preferred, was still overwhelming and frightening.

If you are going through this downsizing process with your person, be aware that this might require a truckload of compassion and patience. Also, take your TIME. Trying to rush someone through the dismantling of their life isn't fair. Include them as much as possible in the process and try to honor their wishes as best you can. (Even though you know that saving that broken teapot doesn't make any sense at all!)

MEDICATION

As an Accidental Caregiver, a very important part of the role is overseeing the various supplements and medications allocated to your person. This is not a small job or responsibility, and it will likely get more and more complicated as time goes on.

If your person can be trusted to manage their own pills and supplements, allow them to maintain this responsibility for as long as possible. Sometimes overseeing their own medication is the last vestige of control they have over their body. Even if they are still involved, you will want to be well acquainted with what they take, when they take it and whether it needs to be tweaked or even just refilled.

Towards the end of her time with us, Mom's health took a dramatic turn and new, stronger medications were introduced. At this point, I felt that I needed to step in and become more engaged in her protocol. This was a hard time. I remember crying when the delivery person first handed me a bag containing morphine for her, and wondering if by giving it to her, I was hastening her demise. Thankfully, it helped far more than it hurt, and got us through a terrible time. As far as I'm concerned, once a person is 97, as my mom was at this time, they get to say what they want, eat what they want and take as many pain medications as are required to keep them comfortable.

There were those who questioned the use of morphine for my mom, which likely contributed to my questioning myself. It is so difficult to know what is best and if you are doing the right thing at the right time. My approach of listening to my heart and soul-centered intuition was very helpful in getting through those uncertain times.

Listening to oneself is important, and listening to and leaning on trusted healthcare professionals is paramount. If Mom pushed back against a recommended protocol, I would engage whoever was suggesting the prescription (primary care physician, nurse practitioner, hospice nurse, etc.) and ask them to explain the rationale directly to her. This worked so well that I'll admit that I may have ascribed some of my wishes and suggestions as coming from the medical team. Guilty as I felt, I'm told that 'therapeutic lying' is a common strategy when helping people make decisions that are undeniably in their best interest.

MENTAL HEALTH

There are two mental states that need to be considered in a caregiving relationship – namely, yours and that of your person. Both are equally important. Many books have been written on this subject, like *The Conscious Caregiver* by Linda Abbit and *Self-Care for Caregivers* by Susanne White, to name a couple. We will hardly scratch the surface here, but I do have a few tried-and-true techniques that were helpful for both me and Mom.

One of the most important concepts that I have learned through years of spiritual and behavioral study and practice, is that we are all solely responsible for our own happiness. You cannot create happiness for someone else. This is a tricky concept for Accidental Caregivers as our *raison d'être* is to create an optimal environment and promote well-being for our people. But well-being isn't happiness – that's up to each of us alone. This is a good reminder as it can be very difficult not to feel like you are failing your person if they are unhappy.

The following are some simple techniques I like to suggest to clients when they are looking to promote a calm state of mind in trying circumstances:

Pause and Breathe

This simple act can save everyone a lot of drama and upset. When confronted with a situation or circumstance that rubs you the wrong way, choose to stop, close your eyes (if possible), and take a big inhale in through your nose and a long exhale out your mouth. Repeat this three times, and I can almost guarantee that you will feel more composed and able to speak from a place of calm rather than annoyance, anger or frustration.

Count to 10

Close your eyes and count to 10 slowly as you breathe in and out of your nose. Nasal breathing connects with the parasympathetic nervous system, which will move you into a calmer, more centered headspace.

Remember Yourself

When breathing deep and counting to 10 won't cut it, the next best thing is to remove yourself. There were definitely times with Mom that I needed to say, "I'm going to leave the room right now and we can talk about this later." Or "I love you, but I just can't engage in this right now." Usually, those times were when I knew that I was past my edge and that no good would come from staying put. Of course, we all know that walking away from someone who is readying themselves for a fight can agitate them further, but again that is their response and not yours to control.

Chanting a Silent Mantra

I fully acknowledge that this may be way out of some people's comfort zones but hear me out. Listening to the same story or, even worse, the same complaint over and over can feel slightly tortuous. My go-to move when I knew that I needed to stay physically present while also protecting a healthy state of mind, would be to mentally repeat a soothing phrase or mantra. It doesn't have to be fancy or spiritual – just any short message that tethers the mind and keeps it from spinning into reaction. Some that have been helpful for me are, "I am here for you", "God provides" and "Om Nama Shivaya". You can try these if they speak to you or spend a minute listening to your intuition and see if anything bubbles up from your own experience and heart.

These are just a few of many strategies available to you. There are also many ways that you can help to support your person's mental health and well-being. If they tend to 'buy trouble' by worrying incessantly and focusing on the negative, gently encourage them to focus on something outside of themselves. I found asking Mom for advice on things going on in my life helped her to feel needed and productive.

Sometimes I would encourage her to move her body in a way that felt good, ask her to list the positive things in her life, or prompt her into talking about her beloved grandkids. Even bringing up lighthearted pop-culture topics, or complimenting her hair or outfit choice, sometimes worked to shift the tone and relieve some of the heaviness.

The best way to promote mental health and a calm state of mind is to operate, as much as possible, from a place of LOVE. If this is the foundation, the ups and downs can be met with grace and the understanding that both people are doing the best they can.

MOBILITY

When Mom first came to live with us, she was fully mobile, though using a cane and occasionally a walker for support. She had long stopped driving, which had been another difficult step in her losing her independence. This isn't uncommon. I've heard so many stories over the years of seniors who resist giving up their driver's license, and whose families have to appeal to their primary physician to formally revoke driving privileges in a bid to keep them from hurting themselves or others.

In the beginning, Mom would join me in running errands and doing the shopping, and she loved the chance to visit a casino. Eventually, leaving the house became too uncomfortable, and the extent of her mobility was trips to the bathroom and navigating herself around the casita. For a time, I would insist on her spending some time out in the yard, until that was no longer an option either.

Movement of any kind is so important for mental health, bone and muscle strength, and efficient circulation. Having spent over 20 years in the yoga and wellness industry, I was committed to keeping Mom moving as long as possible. Thankfully she was, for the most part, a willing participant. She understood the value of exercise and loved to recount how she and her classmates were made to do the same calisthenics in her gym class as the soldiers did during the war. Climbing the rope, scaling the ladder wall, etc. She believed that her longevity was due, in part, to those early years of physical training, and I agree.

Even when she was no longer leaving the house, and sleeping a good amount of the time, we continued to make moving her body a priority. I had a good catalog of easy exercises she could do from bed or sitting in a chair. Even the smallest movements on a regular basis, like ankle circles or stretching, is far better than nothing at all.

MONEY

As I've mentioned, Mom and I set up a joint checking account that I could use to take care of her needs, while she maintained her own checking and savings accounts. Once she was no longer able to get out shopping, Mom discovered the world of home shopping networks. A mixed blessing to say the least. On one hand, she enjoyed being able to still buy gifts for friends and family, and having the packages arrive would brighten up her day. On the other hand, this fun little hobby meant that I was responsible for distributing the gifts, as well as managing any returns, exchanges, etc. Thankfully, we didn't run into the situations I've heard about where seniors are getting scammed or making detrimental financial decisions.

As an Accidental Caregiver, it is likely that one of your responsibilities is to oversee your person's finances and keep their assets safe and secure. This is a great area to have set intentions around so that everyone has a clear understanding and expectation of how things will be managed. Having that conversation at the outset can avoid there being too much resistance when the time comes to monitor the accounts and activity more closely. Mom was able, for a while, to balance her checkbook, look at the statements and make her purchases. That evolved along with everything else, and eventually we both found it simpler if she just told me what she needed, and I would take care of it.

NUTRITION

I love to cook and bake, which was great because my mom loved my food! I know enough about nutrition to know that high protein, low sugar foods are what an aging body needs to remain strong and satisfied. I'm also a firm believer, however, that someone who has made it well into their 90s should be able to eat ice cream for dinner, if that's what they want.

Mom ate what sounded good to her at that moment. Sometimes salmon and vegetables, sometimes just jello and applesauce, and rare days just hot water and toast. She loved baked potatoes, so much so that she requested I put one in her casket with her. We dabbled in probiotics and various supplements to promote gut health, as she struggled with digestion, and I tried as much as possible to give her food from the earth. If there were sweets, I made them myself – except, of course, for her beloved thin chocolate peanut butter cups.

Food is medicine, but on some days eating anything was a win, so I didn't make kale and lentils a hill to die on.

TRANSPORTATION

Getting from one place to another isn't always easy when you are responsible for not only yourself, but someone else's comfort and safety. My mom was able to drive into her 80s, but even though she was still capable, she began to feel nervous. She even had some little panic attacks where she had to pull over to the side of the road. So, even though she still had her own vehicle, it wasn't too long until I was ferrying her around to all her appointments, shopping, errands, and outings.

As for mobility aids, Mom went from using a cane, to a walker, to a 'mobile chair', which is a smaller, lightweight wheelchair that worked well for the days when she was particularly unsteady. There were some outings where I loaded all three 'helpers' into the trunk for her adventures. It was on these days that I was glad to have a vehicle large enough to fit us and all her *accoutrements*. When getting into the vehicle became challenging, I would sometimes enlist my son to help me with loading her in and out.

Once she was no longer willing or able to leave the house, the art of transportation turned into the art of delivery services. Thankfully we live in an age where you can get nearly everything delivered right to your door. At that stage, her traveling required specialized transportation, like the Medi-transport that moved her on a gurney from our home to her assisted living facility.

If your person can still leave the house but is no longer driving, there are a range of transportation services that will come and take them safely from place to place. It may be worth acquainting them with Uber or Lyft, and even doing the first few trips together. In our case, Mom didn't use these services, so I was regularly playing chauffeur. My deep breathing would come in handy as there is a lot of waiting involved when a 40-minute grocery visit takes closer to 2 hours. Have I mentioned that patience is a virtue for us Accidental Caregivers?

"Some people care too much,
I think it's called love."

– WINNIE THE POOH

7

Transition

ONE OF THE FINAL STAGES of being an Accidental Caregiver is almost always one last transition – be it moving your person to a higher level of care, as I did, or saying your goodbyes in their final days. I've been hesitant to share the details of why we had to transfer Mom from our house to an assisted living home as it was an incredibly trying time through which Mom was not herself. I realize, however, that sharing this part of the story may be helpful to those who, like me, don't know about UTI-driven dementia.

One day Mom started to have delusions. At first, they were sort of sweet, like when she reported seeing her mother appear in the hallway. I thought maybe people who had already crossed over were coming to usher her to the other side. These hallucinations quickly became more dramatic, though, with her crying out about "all of these baskets hanging from the ceiling" or that she wanted someone to "turn off that loud music blaring outside!" She became increasingly stressed as she wondered, "What are all of these people doing in my room?!" My family and I spent 48 hours trying to manage her acute physical and mental discomfort, finally agreeing to try the medication Haldol to see if that would help with the delusions. She was still on her anti-anxiety medication, as well as the morphine, and even this scarily strong chemical cocktail had little effect.

Her distress escalated to her hurling diatribes of denigration in my direction. These were some of the hardest moments of my life as I sat trying to hold space for her while being battered with venomous accusations and harsh opinions about my life choices. It was when she threatened to "burn the place down" that I knew I had to act. I called EMS, but their only recourse would be to take her to the hospital, which I didn't want. Our hospice nurse came to the rescue and asked if I wanted to transfer her to the in-unit hospice facility. Through tears I agreed, even though I, along with many others, thought that this would likely precipitate the end of her life.

It did not. After a few days of antibiotics, she was released, and I brought her back home. Although her delirium had been brought on by a urinary tract infection (not an uncommon occurrence for seniors, I learned), I knew that we had turned a corner and that keeping her at home was no longer best for either of us. Fortunately, we were able to secure her a spot in a group home that could provide the full assistance that she required.

She was angry and confused at the decision, but somewhere inside her, I think she understood that I could no longer manage. It took a couple of months for her to settle into the rhythm of the home and accept this new normal, but she did. God bless her. She is now thriving in a way that, despite my very best efforts, she wasn't when I looked after her.

They maintain a healthy routine at the home, and she is cared for by people who have devoted their lives to being Professional Caregivers. Nothing accidental here. Now I visit a few times a week, and she and I have a light, loving relationship where she has only the kindest and most appreciative words for me. I'm thankful that she has no memory of the terrible time that brought on the transition to this place. For the most part, I've processed and accepted the hurt she caused me as just a medically induced 'word salad' that is often par for the course in these scenarios. I've moved past it and can enjoy my time with mom, while also enjoying the freedom of having regained my independence.

"It is not how much you do,
but how much love you
put in the doing."

– MOTHER TERESA

8

Final Thoughts

THE CONCEPT OF TRANSITION is one that I have spent a lot of time contemplating during, and since, my six years as my mother's caregiver. Some days, when you are knee deep in the muck, it feels like the final transition will never come. And then, when it does, you inevitably reflect on the time between the first transition into your home and this last one.

One of the things that has stuck with me the most about taking care of my mom is the mental and emotional dynamic that accompanies the process. At the beginning of this guide, I cautioned you to really consider this decision carefully as it requires a fortitude unlike anything else in life. On one hand, I feel it was a privilege and a blessing to shepherd my loved one through the final stages of her life. On the other hand, it took an undeniable toll on me. Mom would cry and say, "I don't want to be a burden to you all," and I would always respond with "You're not, Mom. We love you." And this was absolutely true. But that doesn't mean that any of it was easy.

I marvel at the hospice nurses who tirelessly care for people like my mom. To me, they are like walking angels. Not only do they perform all sorts of unenviable tasks, but they accept the patients for who they are, all while remaining cheerful and loving. They are true professionals and I am forever grateful for them.

As hard as it was, I am thankful to say that what I have carried away from the experience isn't memories of all the work and worry, but of the beauty experienced in the times between the tasks. I believe the magic and wonder of living lies between the actions of doing. Looking back, I might wish for a do-over on some of the ways I approached this role, but I wouldn't change a thing about the thread of love, and nurturing, and connection that bound all those actions together.

I feel so blessed that I had the honor of taking care of my mom, as difficult as it was at times. My life has seen many different stages, and I can tell you that the satisfaction that comes from the 'daily grind' dance that we all do, is nothing compared to what I received from being an Accidental Caregiver. I love my mother dearly, and being her daughter and her caregiver has taught me an abundance about myself and the life around us. I am happy she is still with us, and I will miss her terribly when she goes.

I hope your choices find you well and that the love for yourself and your person provides strength and support.

"Never believe that a few caring people can't change the world. For, indeed, that's all who ever have."

– MARGARET MEAD

About the Author

Jane M. Mayer

JANE MAYER IS A STUDENT OF LIFE and believes in passing on the wisdom and lessons learned through her unique set of experiences, struggles and personal triumphs. Committed to following her passions, her remarkable career path began with her working as a producer of TV commercials in NYC, where she reveled in the magic of living and working in one of the greatest cities in the world.

Her next step was transformational, as she chose to focus on family and raise her two incredible boys while diving deeply into the world of yoga and wellness. Never one to go halfway, Jane completed her 500-hr yoga teacher certification and taught for awhile before opening her own yoga and wellness centers where she offered classes, workshops, and holistic therapies.

While running her studio, Jane authored and taught a 200-hour yoga teacher training program, as well as produced a series of guided meditation recordings. She continues to teach advanced yoga and philosophy, as well as offer her Postures of Consciousness workshop (based on the 'I AM Yoga' system), at the Southwest Institute of Healing Arts in Tempe, Arizona.

In 2018, Jane combined her entrepreneurial spirit with her passion for cuisine and founded Sweet Jane, an online business offering a variety of delicious gourmet hand pies... made by Jane herself! When she's not doing yoga, running workshops, writing life guides, baking, or cooking for her family, you can find Jane walking her dog Luke, faithfully hitting the gym to promote a healthy lifestyle, and smiling with gratitude for all the amazing experiences life has provided.

"You may not control all the events that happen to you, but you can decide not to be reduced by them.

– MAYA ANGELOU

Acknowledgments

WHERE MY EXPERIENCE OF BEING a caregiver to my mom may often have been a solo act, writing and sharing about it was a mighty team effort.

Love and thanks goes to my partner-in-life, Denis who continues to support me in my ongoing creative efforts while he takes on the responsibilities of financial health for our family. His willingness to take mom into our home without hesitation gave her the opportunity to be safely held and me the efficiency of making it work. It is a wonderful feeling to know when you are loved and I feel that each day.

My gratitude goes to Margi Levitt of The Aspen Press, my faithful web and book designer and friend. I am so grateful for her sticking with me through the process of stops and starts and always being a positive, encouraging, intelligent and creative force to get the job done.

Stacey Dyck who edits the books is someone to whom I was referred by another and turned out to be a gem! Thanks to her for keeping my voice and content, yet making sure all the words were on point.

My old pal from NYC, Bob Giammarco at AE Media, referred me to Steve Harrison who made quick work of our audio recordings by providing a sensitive ear and a super professional experience. I am a lucky person to have such talent available to me.

Writing even a small book as this takes a big effort and one that I do not discount or take lightly. I am so appreciative each day for the flow of ideas and a willingness to put them out into the world for no other reason than to share an experience.

"Life's most persistent
and urgent question is:
What are you doing for others?"

– MARTIN LUTHER KING, JR

NOTES

NOTES

NOTES

www.ingramcontent.com/pod-product-compliance
Lightning Source LLC
Chambersburg PA
CBHW040036110426
42741CB00031B/110